COVID-19
WHAT KIDS NEED TO KNOW

WINNIE CHEONG

Copyright © 2022 Winnie Cheong
All rights reserved.
ISBN: 978-1-922727-30-5

Linellen Press
265 Boomerang Road
Oldbury, Western Australia
www.linellenpress.com.au

Dedication

To my family members. Without your support and contributions this book would not have been completed.

Contents

Dedication iii

Contents v

Acknowledgements vii

Coronavirus Disease 9

Frontline Workers 11

Volunteers 13

Community Cleaners 15

Hospitals and Schools 17

Hygiene and Care 20

Signage and Posters 22

Covid-19 Vaccine 25

Pandemic Impact 27

Acknowledgements

My heartfelt gratitude to our family doctor, nurses and friends who have shared their thoughts and experiences during Covid-19.

Coronavirus Disease

What is Coronavirus Disease?

Coronavirus disease (Covid -19) is a new strain of virus identified in humans. The symptoms include fever, flu, cough, loss of smell, and shortness of breath. Coronavirus is a highly contagious disease and soon there was a pandemic.

What is a pandemic?

A pandemic is an outbreak of disease that spreads very quickly all around the world. A 'pandemic' is a public health emergency.

How does the virus spread?

The virus spreads when people cough or sneeze. We can inhale the virus if we are close to these people. If they cough or sneeze on a surface, we can pick up the virus by touching it.

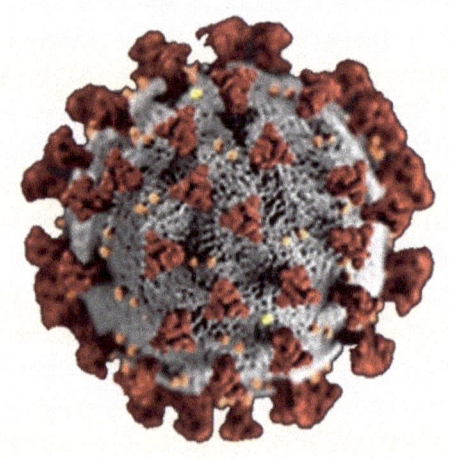

Fact: The first Covid-19 case was reported in Wuhan, Hubei province, China in 2019.

Frontline Workers

Every crisis has its heroes. Doctors and nurses are front-liners who have worked tirelessly to take care of Covid-19 patients since the pandemic outbreak. They are called 'everyday heroes of the pandemic.'

Police officers also play an important role during the pandemic. They make sure people stay home, unless going out for essential needs.

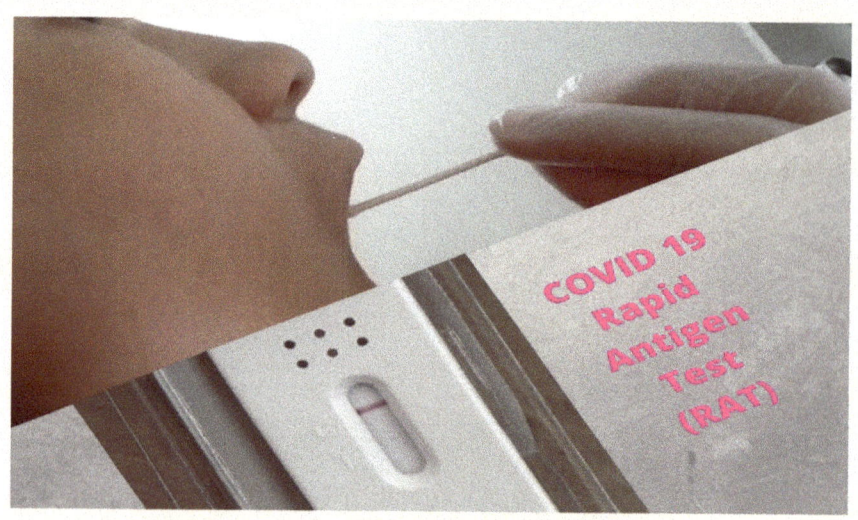

Fact: Dr Kirby White, an Australian physician has developed reusable personal protective equipment (PPE) for doctors.

Volunteers

Volunteers are people who contribute their time and effort to society without getting paid. They help in many areas such as food packing and delivering, cleaning, or being an usher in hospital and train stations.

VOLUNTEERS NEEDED

CARING
LOVE
PASSION
HELPFUL
SUPPORT

DONATIONS WELCOME

CLOTHES
TOYS
KITCHENWARE
FOOD
BOOKS
LINENS

Community Cleaners

Community cleaners play an important role in cleaning and sanitizing public areas such as public transport seats, handrails, door knobs, lifts, community centres, libraries, phone booths, public toilets, etc.

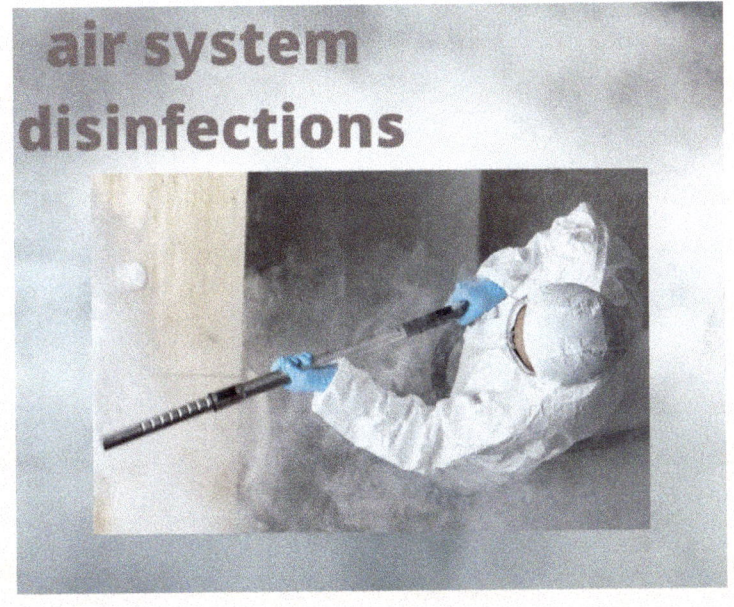

In the supermarket, staff clean shopping carts and check-out counters after each use.

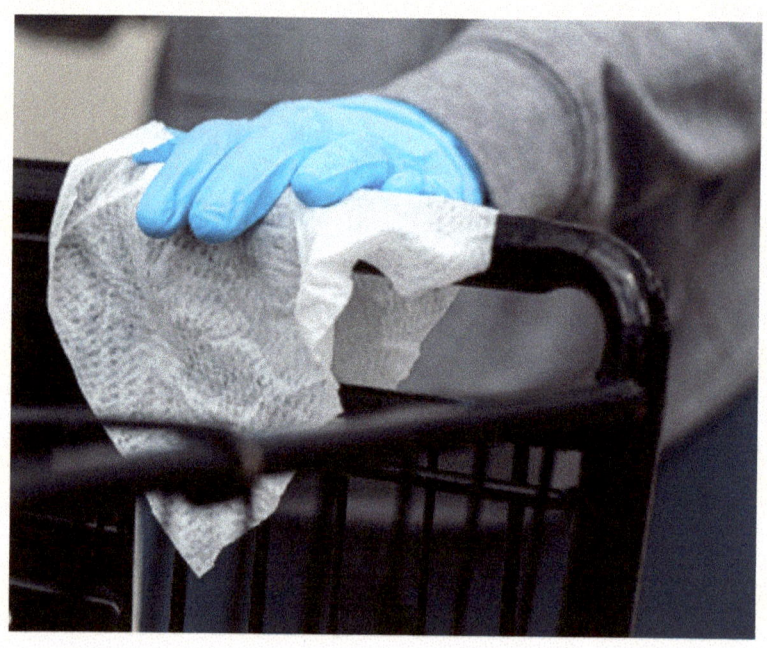

Hospitals and Schools

Hospitals

Some Covid-19 patients need to be admitted to hospital due to severe symptoms. Many hospitals around the world are facing problems of hospital beds shortages, limited PPE, ventilators, etc.

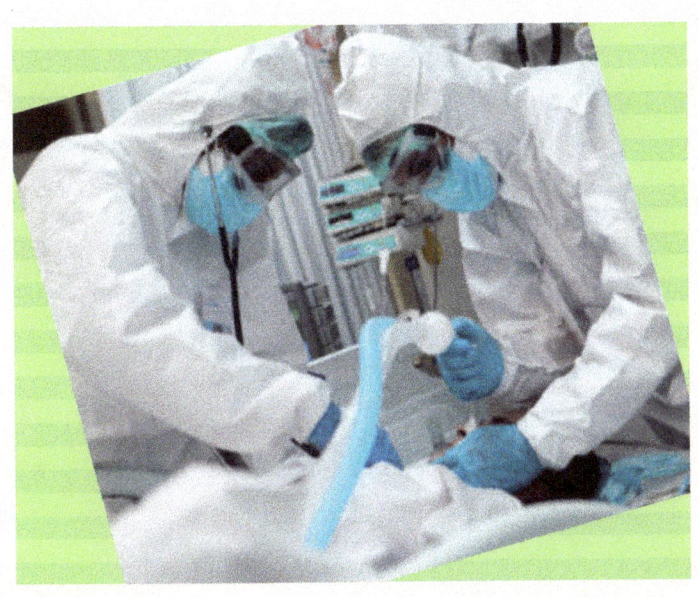

Schools

Schools are sometimes closed during the pandemic. Children stay home to study via internet platforms such as Zoom and Webinars.

Only essential businesses are allowed to operate during a pandemic. These include hospitals, supermarkets, post offices, banks, and pharmacies. Working adults are required to work from home unless they are essential workers.

Hygiene and Care

Disinfectants

Disinfectants are wipes and liquids used to clean our hands and equipment. People use antibacterial wipes, hand sanitizers, and antibacterial spray to disinfect their hands, parcels, and commonly shared equiptment, etc.

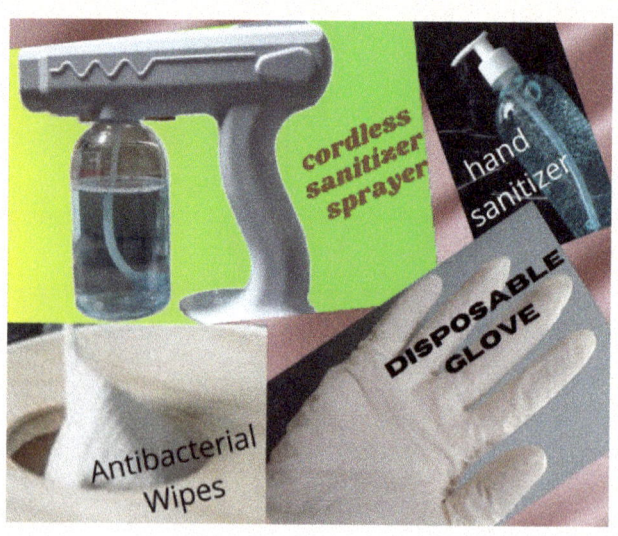

5 easy steps to the perfect wash

wet ~~~> lather ~~~> scrub ~~~> rinse ~~~> dry

Personal Care

People need to wear a mask in public areas and avoid public gatherings. Some people also wear gloves and a face shield while shopping for daily groceries. It is also important to keep a distance from people. We need to wash our hands more often. People use elbow greetings instead of shaking hands.

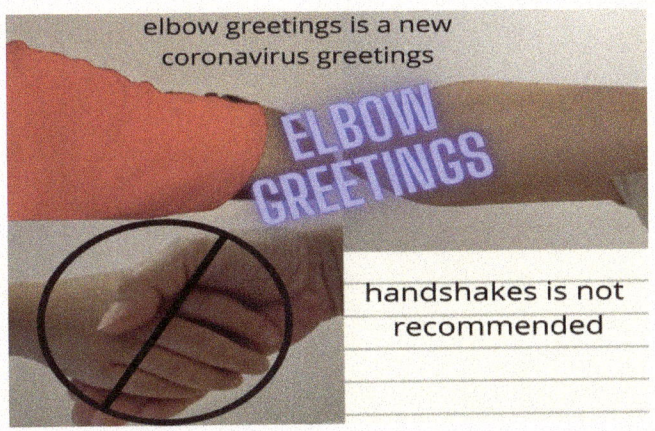

Signage and Posters

Social distancing – avoid mass gatherings and maintain a safe distance

Mask mandatory - people need to put on a mask in the public areas.

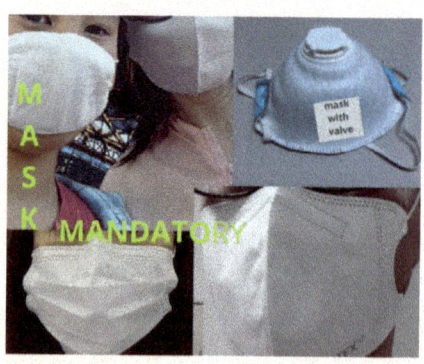

Face shield – this is a shield used to protect our face

 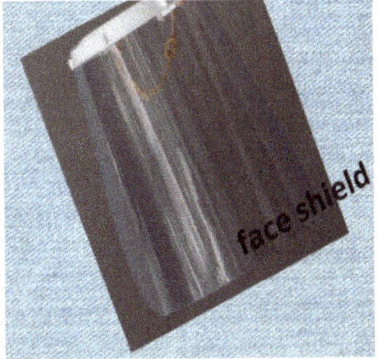

Wash hand – we need to wash or sanitize our hands frequently

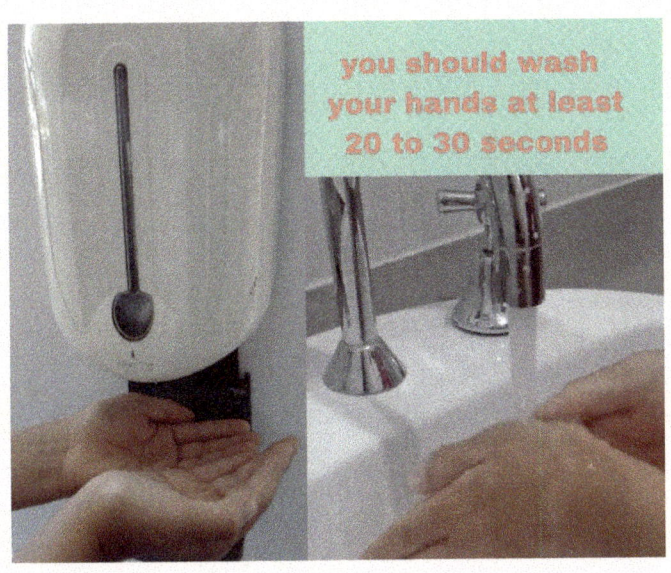

Roll up – get vaccinated to protect yourself and others.

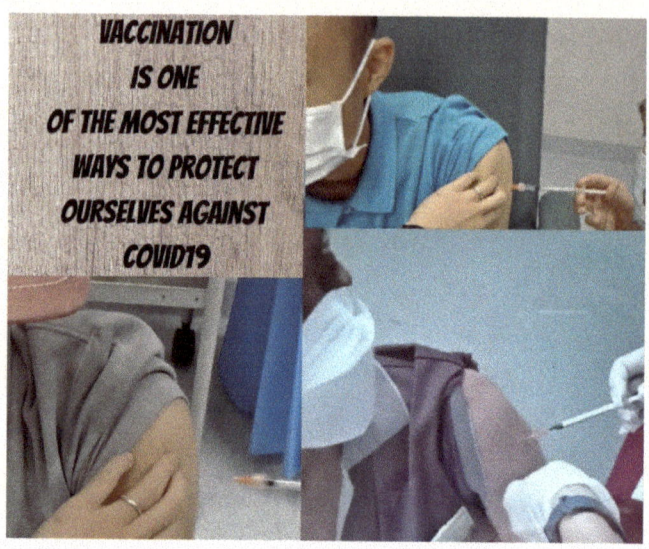

Mandatory contact registration - people need to register their contact details when visiting public places such as supermarkets, restaurants, clinics, government offices, schools, etc.

Covid-19 Vaccine

A Covid-19 vaccine is an injection given to people to protect them from infection. Scientists worked hard to develop the vaccine. The vaccine was finally developed in December, 2020. The vaccination programme has rolled out in many countries since then. People are issued a copy of a digital certificate after being vaccinated. They need this certificate when they travel to other countries in the future.

Most countries aim to achieve 80% of the population immunised before daily routines get back to normal. In December 2021, many countries' vaccination rate surpassed 70%. Obviously, we are on the road towards recovery or a new normal.

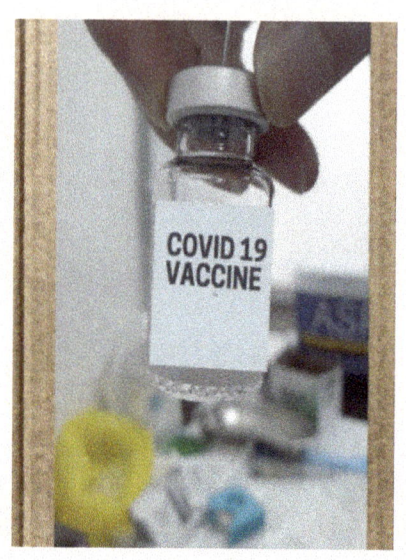

Fact: World first covid-19 vaccine was given to a 91 year old woman in UK

Pandemic Impact

The worldwide Coronavirus pandemic continues to grow. It has caused an enormous impact on our society. 2020 was a tumultuous year in human history, where many businesses closed down. Millions of people lost their jobs. Tourism stopped as international borders closed.

To stay safe:
- Wash your hands
- Wear a mask
- Socially distance
- Get vaccinated

Glossary

business – activity of buying and selling goods

enormous – extremely large or great

essential – necessary or needed

history – the study and record of human past

impact – effect that something has on a situation

international border – a boundary of a country

PPE – personal protective equipment

shopping cart – a trolley used to carry goods

tourism – the practice of travelling for recreation

tumultuous – emotional and disorderly

worldwide – the entire world

About the Author

Winnie Cheong is a freelance writer based in Western Australia.

She graduated with a PgDip in HRM and TESOL. A member of WATESOL, Winnie fluently speaks English, Malay, and Mandarin.

Winnie has worked in human resource planning, media broadcasting, teaching English, and volunteering. She is currently developing her online business THENGLISHUB. This digital learning platform provides all school levels with English learning resources and a mature-age English enrichment program.

She loves travelling, reading, and connecting with people from different cultures. She has travelled to many European countries, the United States, Canada, and countries around Asia. Her vast travelling experience has inspired her to put her extensive knowledge and passion into writing to deliver a constructive message and share it with the wider reading community.

www.ingramcontent.com/pod-product-compliance
Lightning Source LLC
Chambersburg PA
CBHW042000080526
44588CB00021B/2821